ZINDZI, ZAZI & ZIWELENE
MANDELA

SEAN
QUALLS

GRAND MANDELA

Mandela
LEGACY

One day, Zazi and Ziwelene were playing at Grandma Zindzi's house when they found a photograph. It was someone they remembered very well.

"Look, Grandma!" said Zazi. "We found a picture of Grandad Mandela. Can you tell us about him again?"

"Of course," Grandma Zindzi replied. "As you know, Grandad Mandela was my father, but he went to jail when I was only eighteen months old."

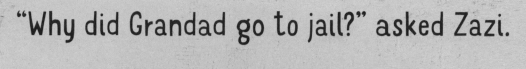

"Why did Grandad go to jail?" asked Zazi.

"He went to jail because he was fighting against apartheid.
Apartheid was a law in South Africa that separated black people
and white people, and said that white people were better.
Grandad was fighting for us all to be equal.

You know like we say, 'I Love You Lots Like Jelly Tots?'
We are different colors but we all taste the same?"
"Uh-huh," said Zazi.
"That's what Grandad Mandela was fighting for."

"Did Grandad have to have his birthday in prison?" asked Ziwelene.

"Yes, but he wasn't allowed to have a party. We had to celebrate it for him outside. Big Mummy still had their wedding cake, which they never had time to cut when they got married.

Every year on his birthday,
she would bring it out, light
a candle, and say a prayer."

"Grandma, where were you when he was in prison?" asked Ziwelene.

"I was left at home in Soweto with Big Mummy and my sister Zenani," said Grandma Zindzi.

"Did you like it?" asked Zazi.

"It was hard. We weren't allowed to live in the same places as white people, and our houses, schools, and hospitals weren't as good as theirs. And when black people and people of color said it wasn't fair ..."

"But why did the white people start making everybody's lives sad?" asked Ziwelene.

"It's because white people were taught under colonization and apartheid to hate," said Grandma Zindzi. "They were taught that they were better than black people."

"Did they make your lives sad too?"
asked Ziwelene.

"Yes," Grandma Zindzi replied. "Every time Big Mummy sent us to school, the apartheid police would come and throw us out. Even if we changed our names and pretended we were someone else, they would still find us.

So when I was five and Zenani was six, some kind people helped us to go to boarding school in Swaziland. We only came home in school holidays to see Big Mummy and the rest of the family."

"That's sad," said Zazi.

"You know Zazi," said Grandma Zindzi, "you don't have to be too sad. Do you know what Big Mummy used to teach us?

She said, 'I don't want to see you cry, because then the enemy will be happy. I want to see you strong, you must hold your head up high.' Big Mummy and Grandad Mandela were strong people because of how they grew up."

"I've got a question about that," said Ziwelene.
"Where was Big Mummy born?"

"Winnie Mandela was born in Bizana, which is near the Wild Coast. She was born among the Pondo people, who produced the best warriors in history!

Grandad comes from the Thembu people.
They are both from royal families."
"Ooh!" said Zazi. "Royal."
"Yes," said Grandma Zindzi.

"Where did Grandad Mandela grow up?" asked Zazi.

"Well," said Grandma Zindzi, "he was born in Mvezo, but he grew up in Qunu."
"I've been there!" said Zazi.
"I know you have," said Grandma Zindzi. "When he grew up, Grandad lived in a traditional home made out of clay with a thatched roof. He had to get water from the river and cook in pots on the fire.

But the lessons that he learnt from his elders made him the man he became—a man who was able to forgive all the people who made him and his family and his people suffer."

"Did Grandad go to school, like us?" asked Ziwelene.

"Yes," said Grandma Zindzi. "When he was older, he studied law. He wanted to learn how to bring about justice in South Africa."

"What is justice?"
said Ziwelene.

"Justice is about people's rights.
It means you have to ask, 'What is
right for everybody? What is fair?'
Grandad didn't think what was
happening in South Africa
was fair."

When white people would tell them that they weren't good enough, they wanted to fight. They thought, if Grandad and Big Mummy could fight and even go to prison to get justice, then they could too."

"Why did the government make Grandad stay in prison for so long?" asked Ziwelene.

"They kept him in prison because they were hoping that the longer he stayed the more tired he would become, and he would give up fighting for his people. But he didn't.

And they hoped that people would forget him and what he stood for, but they didn't. Big Mummy, me, and many other people carried on fighting for freedom. All of these people kept Grandad's spirits alive."

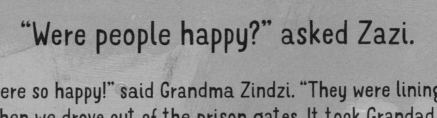

"Were people happy?" asked Zazi.

"People were so happy!" said Grandma Zindzi. "They were lining the streets when we drove out of the prison gates. It took Grandad a long time to get back to Soweto, because all the streets were blocked. It was raining heavily but people were sleeping in the streets, just so they could see him. There was singing and dancing. Everyone was so happy."

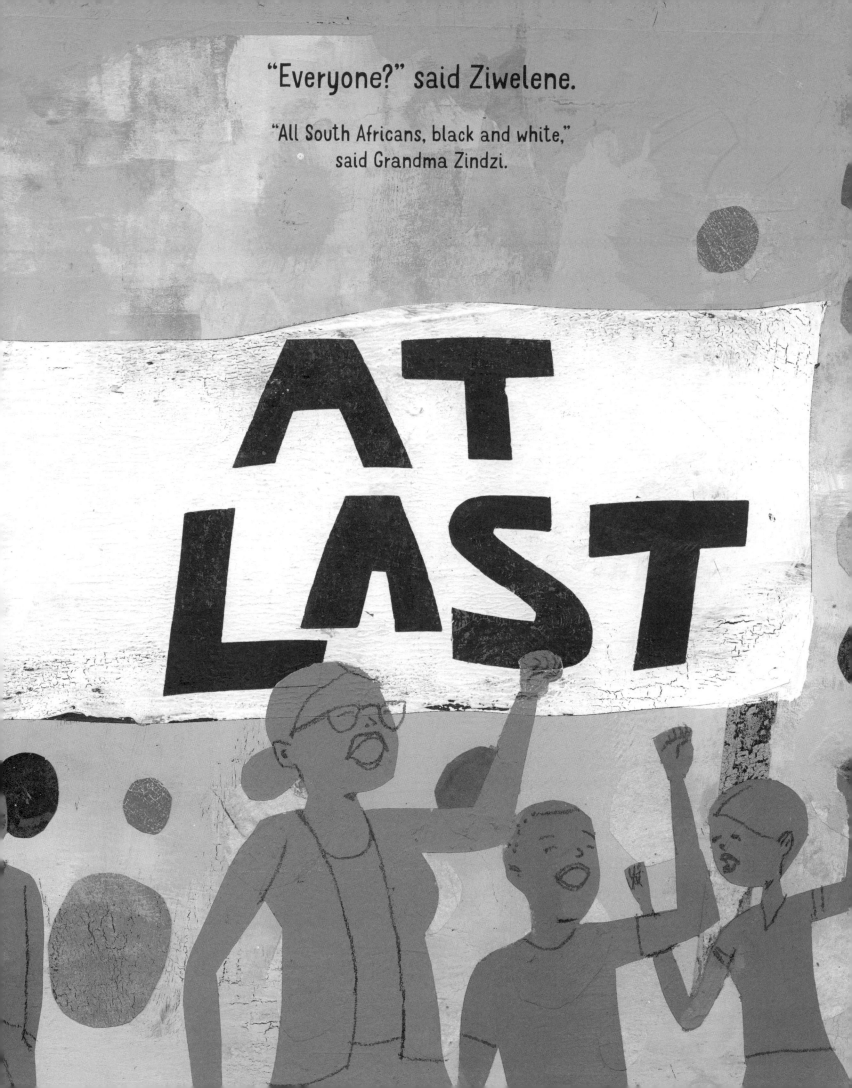

"Everyone?" said Ziwelene.

"All South Africans, black and white,"
said Grandma Zindzi.

AT LAST

"What did Grandad do when he became
President?" asked Zazi.

"The first thing he did was to unite all South Africans.
He reminded us all that we were equal and this is what
we were fighting for: for everyone to live side by side.
No one person was better than another.

He made sure that everybody could go to the same schools, everybody could live where they wanted to live, we could all go to the same hospitals."

"So apartheid was over?" asked Ziwelene.

"That's right. And do you know how he did it? He got his enemies to sit with him around a table."

"That must have been hard," said Zazi.
But Grandma Zindzi had a question for them both.

"Do you know what ubuntu means?"
she asked.

"I think I used to . . ." said Zazi.

"It means, 'I am because we all are'," said Grandma Zindzi.

"This is what we believe as African people: we believe in treating people the way we want to be treated. This is what inspired Grandad to fight for his people, and what helped him to forgive his enemies too."

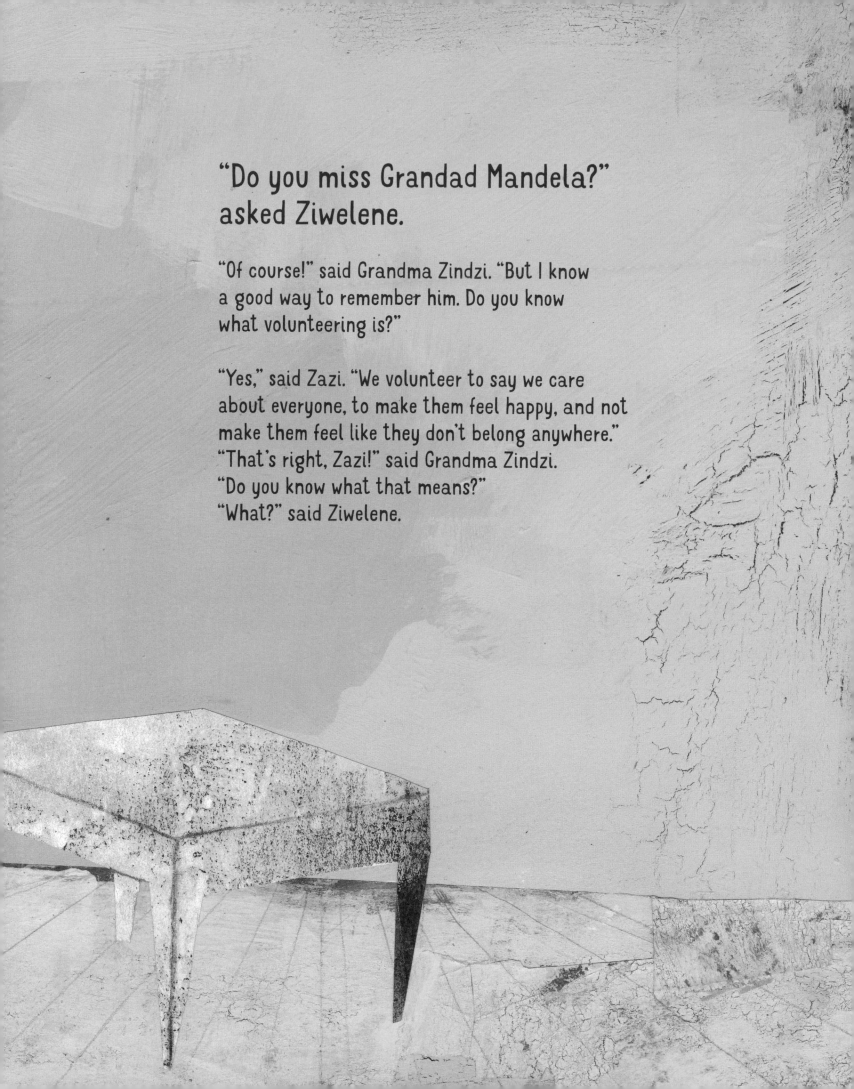

"Do you miss Grandad Mandela?" asked Ziwelene.

"Of course!" said Grandma Zindzi. "But I know a good way to remember him. Do you know what volunteering is?"

"Yes," said Zazi. "We volunteer to say we care about everyone, to make them feel happy, and not make them feel like they don't belong anywhere."
"That's right, Zazi!" said Grandma Zindzi.
"Do you know what that means?"
"What?" said Ziwelene.

"You are both doing the same thing as Grandad Mandela."

Brimming with creative inspiration, how-to projects, and useful information to enrich your everyday life, Quarto Knows is a favorite destination for those pursuing their interests and passions. Visit our site and dig deeper with our books into your area of interest: Quarto Creates, Quarto Cooks, Quarto Homes, Quarto Lives, Quarto Drives, Quarto Explores, Quarto Gifts, or Quarto Kids.

Grandad Mandela © 2018 Quarto Publishing plc.
Text © 2018 Mandela Legacy. Illustrations © 2018 Sean Qualls.
First published in 2018 by Lincoln Children's Books, an imprint of The Quarto Group,
400 First Avenue North, Suite 400, Minneapolis, MN 55401, USA.
T (612) 344-8100 F (612) 344-8692 • www.QuartoKnows.com

The right of Sean Qualls to be identified as the illustrator and Ambassador Zindzi Mandela, Zazi Mandela, and Ziwelene Mandela to be identified as the authors of this work has been asserted by them in accordance with the Copyright, Designs and Patents Act, 1988 (United Kingdom).

ISBN 978-1-78603-136-5

The illustrations were created in acrylic paint, collage and colored pencil
Set in Dodo
Published by Rachel Williams and Jenny Broom
Designed by Zoë Tucker • Edited by Katie Cotton
Production by Kate O'Riordan and Jenny Cundill
Manufactured in Bosnia and Herzegovina by GPS Group

1 3 5 7 9 8 6 4 2

MIX
Paper from
responsible sources
FSC
www.fsc.org   FSC® C110418

Creates, Quarto Cooks, Quarto Homes, Quarto Lives, Quarto

Nelson Mandela was born in 1918 in the Transkei, South Africa. He became famous for his long struggle for freedom for his people from the government-run system of apartheid, which ruled that white and black people had to be separate. His protests against the government eventually led to his imprisonment for 27 years. After his release, he sat down at a table with members of the government to work on a peaceful solution to the fighting, and won the Nobel Prize for Peace. As the first black President of South Africa, he dismantled apartheid, believing that South Africa was a "rainbow nation," with people of all races and colors working together. Nelson Mandela died in 2013, but remains an inspiration to people around the world today.